Orphan among the Irish:
Hanorah's Story

Orphan among the Irish:
Hanorah's Story

PAUL BROWN

ARCHWAY
PUBLISHING

Archway Publishing books may be ordered through booksellers or by contacting:

Archway Publishing
1663 Liberty Drive
Bloomington, IN 47403
www.archwaypublishing.com
1-(888)-242-5904

ISBN: 978-1-4808-0427-2 (e)
ISBN: 978-1-4808-0426-5 (sc)
ISBN: 978-1-4808-0428-9 (hc)

Library of Congress Control Number: 2013921337

Printed in the United States of America

Archway Publishing rev. date: 12/04/2013

This book is dedicated to Nora Martley
(Markley in some family references)
O'Donnell, the author's great-grandmother.

Nora Martley O'Donnell
Circa 1900

Contents

Preface

YOUNG Hanorah was like any other poor girl in 1880s Ireland. Her dream was to one day see America, raise a family, and have the basic necessities of life: food, shelter, and clothes. Love she would provide in abundance. That she knew.

Hanorah kept life vibrant with music and reading. These pursuits and a stubborn hope helped her persevere as she saw her family members perish one by one. Ireland still suffered the effects of *an gorta mor*, the great potato famine, though it occurred a generation before Hanorah's time.

Elder relatives took in Hanorah, orphaned along with her sister, Katie. Life's events eventually carried Hanorah to a new home across the Atlantic. She lived in various circumstances, employed as a restaurant worker, a housekeeper, and a cleaner, and stayed at a convent for a time.

Marriage fulfilled Hanorah's childhood dreams of motherhood—she would have six children—and life on a prosperous farm.

Hanorah was aided by her uncle Finn, her aunt Keira, and her aunt Deidre and by the legacy of others she did not know. She was helped in her quest for a new life by the persistence of local priests, who saw in her a good heart and soul.

This is the story of Hanorah, orphan among the Irish.

Chapter 1

Morning Is What Becomes of It

hANORAh was born into poverty almost a century and a half ago in Ireland, a beautiful island steeped in sadness. From the very first moment that she could remember, she knew who she was and from whom she came.

Her ancestors and her living relatives had their place in Hanorah's heart and gave her a clear identity.

She knew that these people were a part of her makeup. The trees, plants, and flowers that sprouted from the earth started out as tiny seeds, but with the right mixture of sun, air, water, and soil, they grew tall and strong for all to see. Hanorah was a mixture of ingredients—a bit of everyone blended together.

Years later, in a land far from Ireland, she would feel this blend of all her ancestors in the farmhouse where she would live and in the trees planted around it, as only an adult can sense these memories.

Rath de' ort.

Hanorah awoke with these words upon her lips each morning, just as she fell asleep whispering them each night. Translated from Gaelic to the English of her later family, the words mean "The grace of God be with you."

Hanorah's family spoke Gaelic, the language of Ireland. She knew no other language before learning to read, though many of the young people of her village were learning the language of the neighboring island, England. The villagers did not look kindly upon the English. The nuns and the parish priests kept a shaky truce between the two camps.

The faintest agitation could spark fighting. This happened now and again, especially when the Irish lost their homes to the English. The homes were leveled because the Irish had no money to pay the taxes on them. All the Irish were poor. *Apparently the English are rich*, Hanorah thought. *Only the Irish have their homes destroyed.*

Hanorah was starving, and there was little food to fill her belly each morning. This was the normal circumstance for the young girl and her family, the Martleys. They were accustomed to living this way. They understood their fate, one dealt to many people in Castletownberre.

The Martleys had suffered in the past and expected little change in the future. However, Hanorah was like none of her relatives; she always looked at the positive and was sure circumstances would somehow improve. Saint Patrick and Saint Bridget would see to it that life got better. Hanorah stood out among her friends; she carried an aura suggesting that she could change the fate of others. Hanorah felt this too.

Times were not good for the majority of working-class Irish. Many fathers were unemployed, and many families lived with the threat of starvation and death.

Many Irish had become homeless. Large families were often dispersed among relatives who were slightly better off. This diaspora caused a deep sense of loss for all concerned. Many of Irish heritage never got over this loss, even into old age.

Children were the ones most often sent to live with others. There were many mouths to feed, and parents wanted their children to survive. They would use any means necessary to make sure that happened.

Hanorah saw many of her friends lose their homes, which were pulled down before their inhabitants' eyes. She was heartbroken when the father of one of her best school chums was killed while pleading with the levelers to spare his family's home until he could secure funds to pay the taxes. He was crushed beneath stone, sod, and wood, unable to cry for help before the weight halted his breath.

Hanorah, schoolbooks in hand as she passed the site that devastating day, rushed home after class from then on, afraid that her own home might be buried among the stone and the sod and that her own father might be dead.

The Martleys were no different from most families in Ireland in the 1880s. They were poor, hungry, tired, and looking for hope. Ireland was a land of enchanting beauty; the land of Saint Patrick; the land of the shamrock, the symbol of the Holy Trinity, and the land of leprechauns. However, hundreds of thousands of her people suffered. What good was the beauty of the countryside if it brought so little prosperity or hope? Where was Saint Patrick when people were losing their homes? Where were the Father, the Son, and the Holy Ghost when the Irish needed rescue? Where were the leprechauns? Why were no pots of gold left upon the doorsteps of Irishmen? Families lost their firstborn, their second-born, and even their third-born to poverty, disease, and starvation. The Irish felt that God's chosen people in Egypt had not suffered as they did.

Hanorah's parents, Bridget and Brendan, were products of the great potato famine that swept across Ireland in the late 1840s—*an gorta mor*, as Bridget's mother called the tragedy. The famine drove their fathers to America in search of employment to support their families. The two men never returned to their native land, and the dollars sent home in envelopes postmarked from Boston to their starving families eventually stopped appearing.

News reached the Martley and Malone families via a Catholic priest in Boston that both dads were killed in factory accidents. The Irish were considered easy to replace and expendable. There were few safety rules in the factories; the philosophy was that another Irishman would fill the empty slot if the one before him was hurt or killed.

Bridget's family depended on relatives and the meager funds that her mother secured from working in a boardinghouse kitchen. The Malones were poor, but they were not aware that they were.

Brendan Martley was forced to abandon his education at age nine to work in the copper mines. Young Brendan spent twelve hours a day in almost inhuman conditions, but the work meant money for his mother and his siblings. The job was necessary to keep his family alive.

Times remained tough for Hanorah's parents when they were wed at a Catholic parish. The entire town was Catholic. To be any other religion meant that you were not Irish but English or, even worse, Scottish or Welsh. The Irish were not fond of any of these alien groups.

Bridget's mother, Courtney, found comfort in the home of her birth, Sullivan Farm, with her siblings. They would always be a source of strength for her. Fever took her as she tended to her grandkids. Fever was a common ailment in the villages, and medicine was too costly to halt the death march that carried away many people.

Chapter 2

Rath de' Ort

From her earliest years, Hanorah woke up each morning first whispering a prayer, then humming or singing a tune. The songs were lullabies, ballads, and love stories of the land of her birth. Hanorah loved her country, though she did not quite understand the depth of this love. It was not the love she had for her parents or for her siblings. This love was rooted in the earth, in the air, and in the spirit of Ireland.

Hanorah broke into song immediately after she had thanked her Lord for allowing her to see a new day. Family members always heard her intone, "The grace of God be with you," as they too stirred from sleep.

From infancy, Hanorah heard Irish lullabies from her grandmother Courtney, with whom she spent time in Castletownberre, a village not far from her home. She often stayed with her grandmother, since her mother was constantly tending to sickly children. The 1880s were difficult years, even though the copper mines provided employment to many men. The owners did not always pay fair wages, and knew there were always laborers awaiting any job handed to them.

Hanorah was not quite three when her grandmother passed away, but the songs that she sang kept her grandmother present.

Hanorah would recite her prayers in front of a statue of Saint Patrick in the family's one-room cottage. Saint Patrick offered Hanorah hope, for he had suffered as a young person and had been enslaved for many years.

The other statue in the small Martley cottage was of Saint Bridget, a figure quite familiar to Hanorah. She was the Irish saint for whom Hanorah's mother was named at her baptism less than a week after her birth.

The Irish of the 1800s believed that the sacrament should be administered quickly, since an unbaptized child who died would be sent to limbo for eternity. Infant deaths were common, and so almost all Irish parents made this sacrament an immediate priority after a child was born.

Saint Patrick and Saint Bridget gave Hanorah hope for bright days for her family, for herself, and for the land she loved.

Hanorah composed songs in Gaelic, often about loves created in her dreams. She sang about the lush green Irish landscape, the hills and the valleys around her hometown, the nearby river, and the Irish seacoast. Family members were also a frequent subject. Hanorah had a way with words. She spoke little, reserving speech and song for important ideas that came from deep within her heart. She had the voice of an angel sent specially from heaven to sing.

Her ballads kept Aunt Deidre and Aunt Keira rapt. Hanorah highlighted the simple pleasures she enjoyed in their care, including having ample food, her very own blanket, books to read, and animals to play with. These things helped her maintain a positive outlook in times of strife. Her aunts' home in Sullivan Farm was the source of Hanorah's hopes and dreams. It gave her strength and ensured her life.

Besides her parents Bridget and Brendan, Hanorah's family included her siblings Katie, Rian, Fiona, and Lorcan. Hanorah's disposition was always sunny and positive. Her zest for life carried her through many illnesses that did not spare her kin.

She knew that family members who lost the battle to stay alive would find an eternal home in heaven. Saint Patrick would welcome them with a shamrock to symbolize the God awaiting them. Father, Son, and Holy Ghost would be there with Saint Patrick.

Shelter, health, food, and the endless green that blanketed Ireland: these Hanorah associated with her grandmother. She would always hear her grandmother

Courtney's kind words, recall the scent of her grandmother's potato soup, and understand the meaning of the
Gaelic phrase *Rath de' ort* that the elderly lady so often
repeated. Hanorah could sense Ireland in the fragrance
of its seawater and its potatoes.

Fiona was the first to leave the family for heaven. The
angels came as the sun set on the horizon. Bridget and
Brendan were heartbroken. Fever took Fiona after she
had suffered for several days. There was little medicine
and even less money to heal her.

Fiona was not yet two, but her short life had an enor-
mous impact on the Martley family. Her passing left a
hole in Bridget's heart that never seemed to mend. She
lapsed into a melancholy that haunted her for the rest of
her days. Brendan had never taken so much as a sip of ale
but soon found comfort in it. He blamed himself for his
daughter's death and could find no way to make up for
the loss, no matter how much he tried.

Lorcan, not quite four years old, also went to the
Lord one night as fever again swept the family cottage. Bridget's heart was further torn by this second
loss. Rian, then six, Katie, five, and Hanorah, four,
were somehow able to shake off the illnesses that took
their siblings. Hanorah thought she saw a tear fall from
the statue of Saint Patrick the night the angels carried
off Lorcan. She believed that Fiona would now have
company.

The losses aged Bridget and Brendan. Overnight the two soon looked decades older than their real ages. They looked dramatically different to Hanorah. Her mother's beauty and radiance were lost behind a sullen demeanor and glazed eyes. Hanorah's father grew ashen, and his hair turned snow white in color. Bridget and Brendan seemed to be going through the motions of living. They breathed but there was no real life.

Chapter 3

Irish Tunes Her Constant Companions

HANORAH kept a positive outlook despite what life had dealt her family, and the Irish tunes she hummed were her constant companions. They gave her hope. Without them, life might have seemed at an end. These tunes were Hanorah's medication when she and other family members were ill. Hanorah dreamed that her tunes could bring Fiona and Lorcan back to the family cottage. She wrote songs about her lost siblings and hummed these tunes to her mother when she saw her fall into melancholy. The tunes were medicine for her mother. Bridget's face would light up and a twinkle would return to her green eyes. For just a moment, she would radiate the beauty she had in a better time—before marriage, before children, before her losses.

Hanorah would leave the cottage each morning in search of water. The cottage was by no means a good residence, even in the Ireland of the 1880s. It had a thatched roof, dirt floors, rock walls, and few furnishings. The old water pot that Hanorah carried held several gallons. It was one of the Martleys' most prized possessions, for without it, they would not be long for the world. The family depended on the water for drinking and cleansing. The water pot held an honored place in the cottage between the statues of Saint Patrick and Saint Bridget.

The Martleys slept on straw strewn across a portion of the cottage floor, sharing the three blankets they owned to keep warm at night.

Fleas and bedbugs were always a nuisance in the cottage, and Hanorah dreamed of the day when she would be free of bug bites and have a floor made of wood. Her friends lived as she did, with straw floors and constant bug bites, but she knew her relatives in Sullivan Farm had wooden floors, rock walls, and no fleas or bedbugs. Hanorah loved going to Sullivan Farm, though she missed her parents when she was there. She dreamed of the day her parents would have more than meager possessions.

Hanorah knew she would have her own blanket when she stayed with Uncle Finn, Aunt Deidre, and Aunt Keira. Each of these three relatives was a singular character, as Hanorah would one day discover about her uncle.

The three were Hanorah's grandmother's siblings. They managed the family farm and were not married. They were known as the old maids and "bachelor man." People assumed that the two sisters were happy living single and that their brother enjoyed bachelorhood. This was not an uncommon vocation for many members of Irish farm families. The church always took a sibling as a priest or a nun, and others often stayed home until old age took them, content with the single life.

Uncle Finn had a secret that his sisters eventually discovered: he had been married many years before Hanorah or even her parents were born. Finn had wished to take this secret to his grave. However, pen and paper betrayed him. Had he not had a penchant for writing, his secret might have been buried with him.

Hanorah loved her aunts and her uncle, and she was often sent

Keira

to stay at their farm, especially when her mother suffered from melancholy after losing two children.

Melancholy was the fate of many mothers of Hanorah's friends, and she assumed this condition could be attrib-

<u>Deidre</u>

uted to birthing too many babies. Most of those mothers, however, were suffering because of the loss of so many of their children. Many mothers died in childbirth. Hanorah did not want her mother to have any more children, fearing God might take her too. She did not understand how babies were made, and had she been aware of the facts of life, the nuns would have chastised her for knowing too much too soon.

Hanorah's grandmother and two of her siblings were dead. God needed to leave a few people in Ireland alive, she thought. He should not take everyone she knew to his home in heaven.

How did Hanorah view herself? She knew that she had been born in the 1870s and was Roman Catholic. She thought that she would one day live in America and sing to crowds for money. Hanorah dreamed of the day her songs would be heard in Boston and New York City. All she had to do was make the dreams a reality.

Hanorah was a child of Ireland, shaped by her family's pain and the suffering. She was a composite of the personality traits of all of her ancestors. From this she seemed to draw the perception of a wise owl.

<u>Finn</u>

Hanorah seemed to know every family member well and could see the good qualities in each. She tried to overlook those traits that might get on the nerves of others, the character flaws that might cause these relatives to be shunned in one way or another.

Tempers often got heated at large family gatherings, and redheads were said to be the likeliest to lose their cool. Hanorah knew this was a myth, because she was blessed with flaming red hair and was not prone to arguments. Appearances were often fodder for myths, but Hanorah was not an easy target.

Hanorah would look to the green countryside and to the seacoast and compose songs in her solitude. She wrote them in Gaelic and loved to practice singing her creations to the birds that drifted down to the green fields or to the goats and the sheep in the countryside. These were captive audiences.

The birds and the sheep would not criticize Hanorah's compositions, and she gained strength from the Irish landscape. The smell of the salt air on the coast invigorated her spirit and channeled her thoughts into the tunes she would sing. Hanorah seemed to be the only Martley to have this free spirit, and she thanked Saint Patrick and Saint Bridget for this disposition each day in prayer. Her lyrical works were written in her mind, since paper and pencil were available only at school. These items were costly, and money couldn't be wasted on frivolous things. It was needed for food.

Hanorah had a remarkable memory for every song she created. Her memory was sharper than the end of a seamstress's best needle, and no detail large or small escaped her eye. She recorded images as if she had a photo gallery in her mind and Kodak was shooting the pictures. The memories included the lyrics to the songs she composed.

Ireland was blessed with gifts that might have been its redemption, but it was cursed in other ways. God gave Ireland breathtaking beauty but forgot to give its people material wealth or enough food. This was especially clear once the potato blight hit the land. Faith taught the Martleys that hard times would end through the intercession of Saint Patrick and Saint Bridget. Somehow, there would one day be prosperity for Ireland—or at least for the Irish who had left their native land.

Years later Hanorah would find the time to write down the music and the lyrics to her songs before she too passed from the earth. These songs, found many years later, were among her few possessions. She had little, since there was often no money even to purchase food. Her possessions after a lifetime could be counted with the fingers on two hands.

Hanorah's family was poor, as were most others in their town. Villagers who wanted to prosper realized that they had to leave the land of their birth to do so. Death would often find them before they could make the move. Many ailments stalked the village, and a perpetual sense of loss hung over the place. Prayer was people's only solace, save for the beauty of the landscape. God gave much suffering to the Irish, but he blessed them with a wonderful world as far as the eye could see. Perhaps this visual blessing was a sign from God that the Irish were destined to spread across the face of the earth and bring their humor, their spirit, and their religion to others. Only God would know this answer, or perhaps Saint Patrick and Saint Bridget.

Chapter 4

Nature, a Gift That Blessed Ireland

IRELAND was beautiful, and the island's southwest, where the Martleys lived, was green, hilly, and blessed with a lovely coast. A river near their town provided fresh water. Perhaps Ireland was blessed with natural beauty to make up for its lack of financial wealth. Certainly there was little among most of the people in the countryside and in the villages.

One of the few sources of wealth, copper mining, seemed to be polluting water near Hanorah's village, and Brendan believed this was part of the reason for his family's medical troubles. The long hours of mine work diminished his hearing, impaired his vision, left him fatigued, and caused him to suffer recurrent diarrhea. Brendan's respiratory problems grew worse the longer he mined, and he worried that his family would suffer these ailments. He needed to work to support his family, and for years he could suffer in silence. This was part of being a man for the Irish of that era. But as his health grew worse, he was unable to hide his medical condition from family members.

Hanorah loved Sundays in her hometown. The Martleys would walk hand in hand to the Catholic church at six in the morning. After Mass, Uncle Finn would take Hanorah and her sister Katie off to spend the day at Sullivan Farm. Uncle Finn, Aunt Keira, and Aunt Deidre were central to the Martley family's life.

Rian was always too sickly to accompany the girls to the farm, but Hanorah would bring home a treat for her brother after her Sunday visits. This would often be a piece of bread, a slice of cake, or a special potato. Everyone in the Martley family saw food as a gift.

Rian

Food would have been scarce for the family if not for Sullivan Farm. Food always seemed to be plentiful at the farm. Hanorah loved this about the place.

Hanorah dreamed that one day she would have her own farm and that she would have children. There would be ample food at this farm, enough so her children would see decades of life and not meet the fate her siblings met.

Hanorah's dream of singing the songs she composed would finance this vision of her future world.

After visiting Sullivan Farm, Hanorah and Katie often took home a burlap bag filled with potatoes. The potatoes were rationed carefully and could provide the family nourishment throughout the week. Hanorah was forever grateful for these gifts. Uncle Finn was the master cook on Sundays and always served chicken, potatoes, and bread for lunch. Chicken was a treat for the Martley sisters. Aunt Deidre said the chicken would keep them healthy if they ate it regularly. The Martleys had no funds for such pleasures, but Sullivan Farm was overrun with chickens.

The Sunday meal at Sullivan Farm was the feast of the week, and the only time the girls would eat something other than potatoes or bread. Chicken was delicious, especially roasted as Uncle Finn prepared it. This was one of his specialties, and he was noted for it around town as much as he was for his brew.

Aunts Deidre and Keira loved the Sunday meal too, for it was the only one they were not required to prepare. The two sisters, however, contributed by baking something fresh the day before. They refused to do any cooking on Sundays. This was their day of rest, the duo would repeat time and time again. "God rested on the seventh day, and so too shall we!" The sisters loved to repeat this line to their brother.

The two were prone to giggle at each other's words, and their hearty spirits made them the best of companions for Hanorah. She loved their zest for life. Even at an advanced age, they were still happy, still cheerful, still so full of the Irish spirit. Villagers often said the sisters could never meet men able to keep up with them, which is why they never married.

Hanorah and Katie would savor every morsel of the cakes and pies their aunts baked. The girls believed they were in heaven at Sullivan Farm. The two-story cottage had wooden floors, furniture, and lots of rooms; chickens, goats, and sheep were everywhere. There were also two cows. Deidre and Keira loved milk, and Katie and Hanorah drank it on every visit. The girls sometimes even got to eat eggs, one of Hanorah's favorite foods. Her aunts scrambled them in a pan filled with potatoes. This was a treat!

Hanorah loved the family room on the first floor because one wall was given over entirely to bookshelves from floor to ceiling. The shelves were stocked with books on every subject. Hanorah thought she was in heaven with this multitude of books. They unlocked all sorts of doors and fueled her dreams. A book took her away from her drab life and transported her to a different world.

She took to reading as a fish takes to water. Hanorah knew nothing of her aunts or her uncle, other than that they were kind to her and her family. That is, she knew nothing of them until stumbling one day upon a dusty book handwritten but legible.

The writing was all in Gaelic, which she could read fairly well. The nuns at her parish school had seen to it that all students mastered reading and writing and arithmetic by Hanorah's age, no matter their circumstances.

As she started thumbing through the aging pages, which crumbled and flaked a little as she turned them, Hanorah understood that this was a journal written by Finn Sullivan years before. The pages contained information that Uncle Finn must have secretly wanted revealed, though not necessarily in his lifetime.

Hanorah discovered what she thought to be a hidden treasure in the journal's pages. The treasure was a sealed envelope with the words "For America" written not in Gaelic, but in English. Underneath this was a second line that read, "To be opened by finder only." This envelope would be the key to a new world. The key was not to be used just yet, though.

Uncle Finn wrote about a time in his life that he had shared with no one. Surely, Hanorah had never known about it. Surely, her mother had not, nor her grandmother years before. What she read enthralled her and gave her an even greater thirst to leave Ireland for America. The journal told tales of her uncle's days as a sailor, tales of his love life, and tales of the family that Hanorah had never heard. Uncle Finn recounted his travels in Asia,

Africa, South America, Australia, and the European continent. He had also been to Boston, New York City, Philadelphia, Richmond, and New Orleans. There were tales of love and money, tales of heartbreak, and tales of soul-searching.

Finn bared his soul in the journal, most likely long forgotten by the author. Uncle Finn was old and wrinkled with rumpled clothes—a little like the journal, Hanorah thought.

The journal told of episodes in Uncle Finn's life unknown to anyone else in Sullivan Farm, it seemed. Finn had lived a life away from the village and had traveled the world and seen many places far from Ireland. Reading the journal, Hanorah discovered many traits that her uncle must possess but had not revealed. She was enthralled and enchanted and could not put the journal down even to eat. Eating was something Hanorah was sure to do if food was available, but the journal contents were delectable, each word a precious morsel.

This fascinating journal gave Hanorah courage. She believed that she too could one day leave behind the poverty that dominated her life. She could leave the Ireland that she loved so much but that perhaps did not love all of its people. Uncle Finn had not lived on this farm all his life but had gone places most of the Irish of his era had not known even existed. Hanorah too could go off to other destinations across the earth.

Chapter 5

Somewhat of a Legend, It Was Thought

UNCLE Finn preferred his own homemade brew concocted from grains, which the girls could see fermenting in a barrel kept in the Sullivan Farm house basement. This was his beer, and he was also known to be a winemaker of sorts.

Finn served the beer at a weekly card game with old friends. A hand of cards with friends from his childhood always meant a bottle of Finn's froth, as his graying buddies called the brew.

The local parish priest was known to have a sip or two of Uncle Finn's brew when not celebrating Mass or performing his other duties. It helped him relax from the pressures of scribbling sermons, hearing confessions, visiting the sick, and instructing his parish flock in the catechism.

The wine, which Uncle Finn also made in the basement, was intended for use at the parish. It would become the blood of Christ at Mass, and the good father was forever thankful to his friend for this gift.

The portion of the wine not gifted to the church would go to Finn's sisters and to his neighbors as presents for holidays or special occasions. Uncle Finn became noted for his bottled brews and was highly regarded as a man of many gifts.

Besides his skill at making wine and beer, Finn was known across County Cork for his storytelling. He was somewhat of a legend. At least that's what he told folks, and friends believed him. Who could doubt a man who could mesmerize a crowd and seemingly awaken the dead? Finn had a knack for keeping listeners in awe of him. He seemed to have this effect wherever he went.

Who was Uncle Finn? Hanorah wondered. She was eager to read the journal from crinkled page to crinkled page because she felt she was a composite of relatives living and deceased and might learn

Kilmer in youth

something about herself as well as about him. Uncle Finn was the youngest of twelve siblings and was the only male among the brood. He had no chance to secure a bride from the Sullivan Farm area, since his eleven sisters would not hear of their brother's affections being wasted on another lass. Finn's fate seemed to be sealed at his birth: being controlled, as he would note in his journal, by "eleven cackling hens." He mentioned this in his storytelling.

Hanorah knew she could not reveal the journal's contents to a soul. Apparently no one had known the journal existed except Uncle Finn, who must have thought he had lost it long ago. The journal and the envelope that accompanied it were apparently sent to Hanorah by Saint Patrick himself.

Hanorah was familiar with Uncle Finn's traits, but the rest of his life was a mystery until she found the journal. She did not place it back on the shelf until she had completed the last page. She noted

Kilmer in old age

the exact spot where she gingerly reshelved the journal. Hanorah wanted to read it again and again.

At the ripe old age of fifteen, Finn ran away from the home ruled by the cackling hens and went off to Dublin to pursue what he hoped would be a better life. He thought it time for the single rooster of the household to escape twenty-two watchful eyes.

His sisters were well meaning, Finn knew, but too often they smothered him. He needed to breathe and to express himself, and he had to leave home to do it. He needed independence from Sullivan Farm. Finn believed that he was already a man and that he could face any obstacle that came his way. He was ready for the unexpected, whatever it might be. Had Finn not faced eleven older sisters and survived? He had indeed, and he left Sullivan Farm vowing never to take a bride. She would only turn into someone like his sisters, Finn believed. He longed for a life away from twenty-two marching feet and from eleven mouths that never seemed to be still. All eleven sisters would constantly cluck orders at him. No more of this for Finn. There had to be another life outside of his village. He was ready to fly this chicken coop. He was henpecked as only a rooster could be.

The journal had to be keeping a secret. The first four pages showed a person lost in mundane thoughts. Hanorah herself was this way much of the time, since she loved to daydream.

The secret was revealed on page five. When Finn had pledged at age fifteen never to take a bride, he had good intentions, but he had not yet experienced the effects that hormones eventually have on a boy's body. He would not be able to keep his vow.

As Hanorah continued reading, she discovered a relative she had never heard of before: Uncle Kilmer. In Dublin, Finn wound up in the home of an aged kinsman who needed someone to tend to his infirmities. The elderly Uncle Kilmer was happy to have a relative come to stay with him. Kilmer had become prosperous over the years but shunned by his Irish family. His crime was to marry an English girl and to leave the Catholic faith to become Anglican.

The villagers back in his hometown called Kilmer names. His family ostracized him from the day he set foot under the roof of the English girl. Their love was not planned. It just happened, as love sometimes does under some conditions.

Kilmer never regretted his marriage to the English lass, but he would later say, "I am forever a shadow of the missus, I am!" And he was. Her death would leave a void to be filled. Kilmer was without his dear departed wife. He missed her. But he had spent a lot of years with his missus before she left the earth. They were good years.

Kilmer's name was no longer brought up by his Irish family except among the brave few unable to fathom the logic for his excommunication. His crime was marrying outside of the Irish, outside of their faith, and outside of the Irish village of his birth. With these three strikes against him, Kilmer could never be absolved. He always felt the loss of his Irish ties, though he grew wealthy beyond his dreams. He doubted he would have become such a great success had he remained at home. But he did not dwell on any injustices against him. Instead, he spent his time working and prospering.

Finn had overheard his eldest sister talk of Kilmer one day. Kilmer was Finn's father's brother, but Finn was not aware of the prejudice entrenched in many a home. Being the baby among twelve, he couldn't recall meeting his uncle. Deidre, the eldest, knew the clan's history well. Finn never knew of his uncle's existence until he overheard her conversation. The family acted as though this relative was deceased. The few pictures of Kilmer were used as cooking fuel in the kitchen stove. The fire cleansed relatives of his memory, or so they thought. But this was far from the truth.

The ostracized Uncle Kilmer walked on a two-way street of prejudices. His English wife's family wanted nothing to do with the Irish. The Irish were considered trash, unworthy of humanity. Kilmer's wife told many of her friends that her husband was a Scotsman, and Kilmer identified himself this way for many years. She too was embarrassed over his heritage. Though she loved him dearly, Kilmer's wife had to convince herself that he was a Scotsman, not an Irishman. Kilmer accepted this fate. He thought life was much like a game of cards: the luck is in the draw. Life can deal out many cards that you might not like, and you win some games and lose others. There are good days and bad days in life. You must accept reality.

Kilmer's wife died in a train accident. He was injured and left unable to walk. His considerable wealth enabled him to employ a housekeeper, but he wanted to return to Sullivan Farm one day. His family might forgive him for his marriage and his change of faith. Perhaps a trip to the parish priest and a visit to confession might secure forgiveness among his kinfolk before he died. Kilmer believed he could receive more help from the Virgin Mary than from Saint Patrick. He prayed his rosary daily and had faith that his prayers would be answered before he died.

Finn's appearance brought the family back to him, if only for a while. The fifteen-year-old standing at his door was the answer to his prayers, Kilmer believed.

Finn became devoted to his great-uncle, working for him as a helper day and night. Finn took to Kilmer as a son would to a father. Kilmer was childless and loved the boy as only a father could. He was happy that this youth was not prejudiced by others in his family. Kilmer had heard all the incredible stories fabricated about him over the years by his village kinfolk.

The tales were told because of his union with an Englishwoman. He heard these stories from business acquaintances who traveled now and again to the home of his birth. The stories turned Kilmer into a creature part devil and part dragon. The fabrications grew more colorful as the years turned into decades. The burning of Kilmer's pictures enabled the mythmakers to add unflattering details to his appearance: a snaggled tooth, pointed ears, a crooked face, a long nose, gray eyes, and fiery red hair ablaze with heat.

Finn felt a kindred spirit between himself and his uncle, and a special bond was formed, as only family can sense such a connection. Finn had never known his father and barely recalled even an image of his mother, so he was happy to have a parent figure rather than his sisters ordering him around. Finn was old enough to take on his own identity and needed a role model to help him. Since he had no father, his uncle would do just fine as a substitute. Finn felt himself a man at fifteen, but deep in his heart, he wanted to be a boy a bit longer. Kilmer let him do that.

Finn spotted a young beauty one day. She had fair skin and a complexion as silky as the finest linen. Her eyes were as green as a shamrock and her hair as red as elderberries in the fields. Finn had vowed not to marry.

He wanted no part of a wife or children, only riches. Why had this lass crossed his path? This was not what he had moved to Dublin to find.

Why did his heart start pounding and his skin begin sweating every time he saw this beautiful girl? Finn was not himself when she was in the vicinity.

He saw Carrie as he pushed Uncle Kilmer to an Anglican service in his wheelchair one sunny Sunday morning. Carrie's body language was as evident as Finn's at this meeting. She was shy and quiet, but clearly had an eye for Finn. He was several inches taller than most lads his age. He was lean but not skinny with green eyes and a crop of reddish-blond hair that quickly caught Carrie's attention.

The two felt an immediate attraction to each other. It was love at first sight. They believed that they were destined for one other.

Finn stood out in a crowd as a lit candle would in a darkened room. Carrie had seen him during hurling matches. He stood out as one of the finest players on his team. Finn was a hurling fanatic and played the sport constantly in his spare time. Hurling was much loved in Dublin, and Kilmer loved to watch the matches.

Kilmer attended many hurling matches with Carrie steering his wheelchair. Kilmer's presence ensured that the two love-struck Irish kids would be kept a respectable distance from each other. A chaperone was a requirement for those young and in love in Ireland during that era. Boundaries had to be respected, and the relationship had to be respectable. That was it.

Realizing that the two teens were drawn to each other, Kilmer was kind to both and kept watch over his young nephew. Uncle Kilmer chaperoned all visits that the couple made, and never were the two to be left unaccompanied. They believed themselves capable of being left alone, but this was not to be.

Scandal would not befall his nephew or Carrie. The town was quick to shun those regarded as morally unfit, and the ban would last a lifetime. Kilmer would not allow others to shun his nephew in any way. Finn was to connect with others in social and family circles. The future of his young charge rested in his hands, and Kilmer would see to it that nothing untoward took place.

Finn was not Kilmer's son, but he grew to feel that the boy was a good substitute and that the future must only be good for his nephew. Many an Irish lass was ready to take a husband to spare her parents another mouth to feed. Carrie might be one of these girls, Kilmer thought.

Finn might be a ticket out of her parents' home. Kilmer had business connections not only in Dublin but in Belfast, and it was known in the social circles of both cities that Finn would someday inherit his uncle's considerable wealth.

Uncle Kilmer lived his life in scandal. Not allowed to be among the Irish, not allowed to be among the Catholics once he became Anglican, and not accepted by his English wife's family or by the Anglicans, he was the object of ridicule. Somehow, though, his wealth grew because of the scandal talk among Dublin residents. Kilmer's business prospered in Belfast even more so than in Dublin. For all of his other problems, the business brought him name recognition and wealth and a sense of satisfaction. His family had forsaken him, but the regular citizens had not.

Kilmer's business was brewing adult beverages: ale or beer, and wine. This business prospered and included related business operations that were involved in this ale and wine dealings. Transportation, marketing, bottle manufacturing, real estate.

Finn learned the business well in a short time, and this business expertise would serve him a lifetime.

Most knew nothing of his past, and he would not volunteer the facts. The local newspapers often asked Kilmer if they could write long stories about his life and his success. He acknowledged this press with a few quips and quotes and allowed the papers to photograph him. The life he had forsaken would not be public news. His life was own, and it was meant for living, he thought.

Falling ill one cold winter day, Kilmer told Finn to be happy in life and take Carrie as his bride. Carrie was

Irish, Catholic, and beautiful. Kilmer told Finn he could see that the two were in love. He gave Finn his blessing for marriage, for what that blessing was worth. "May the luck of the Irish be with you in life," Kilmer told his nephew.

Carrie and Finn married when Finn turned eighteen; Carrie not quite seventeen. The wedding was witnessed by the entire parish, and Uncle Kilmer was happy to see that his protégé had secured a happy life. Kilmer sat in the front pew, content at last and feeling that his life had some purpose after all. He was proud of his nephew, proud to have given him a future, and honored to be in the front row for the wedding celebration. Kilmer's happiness was long in coming and short in duration.

The day after the wedding, Uncle Kilmer passed away in his sleep. He was seventy-six, it was discovered upon his death. Carrie and Finn learned of his passing a week later after returning from their wedding trip to Limerick. Finn felt alone in some ways with the sudden loss of his beloved uncle, but he believed that Kilmer's quiet passing signaled acceptance of his union, which the old man had blessed before going home to see Saint Patrick and the Virgin Mary, his preferred saint.

Kilmer left his wealth to Finn, as most in the community had anticipated. Finn decided that he would set out for a new life in America. The inheritance was substantial. Kilmer, also a resident of Belfast after doing business in that city for many years, had considerable assets there as well as in Dublin.

Carrie was a great source of knowledge when it came to money. She figured the funds left to Finn belonged to both of them. Finn was all too eager to entrust his beautiful bride with the responsibility of keeping all the money coming in from the sale of businesses and properties and holdings around the country. The amount was more than Carrie imagined in her wildest dreams.

Carrie also discovered not two months into the marriage that she was with child. She had not planned to become a mother this soon after her wedding. Carrie did not intend to tell her husband the news, and fortunately for her, she knew she could maintain a trim figure for the duration of her secret plan. Her husband would not be a part of her scheme. His funds, however, would be. She thought no one would be aware of the body forming and changing her on the inside. Somehow this would have to be kept quiet.

The newlyweds intended to use the inheritance to move to America and start their own business there. Finn was happy to please his bride, who wanted to leave Ireland as quickly as they could. Money, more money, even more money: Carrie told Finn to keep the estate funds flowing her way. "Sell everything for cash!" she would encourage her husband.

Carrie prepared for the trip to America, while Finn sold his uncle's homes and businesses in Dublin and in Belfast. He learned of many other holdings that Kilmer had scattered about Ireland. Finn was surprised at how enterprising his uncle had been. He gave all the funds from the sales to Carrie to hold for the passage to America. Finn met with Irish friends also intending to emigrate. His entire hurling team anticipated leaving with Finn for America, the passage paid for through his generosity.

Finn was still in the dark about Carrie's pregnancy, and she shared the fact with no one. The English doctor who gave her the news was the only other person who knew. Carrie figured the doctor would not cross paths with Finn. Her husband's absences to do business gave Carrie many chances to design clothes that would hide her size. Her figure was kept almost the same, and in darkened evenings Finn was no more the wiser. The pregnancy stayed a secret. Carrie was clever, very clever—conniving, in fact.

Finn was occasionally required to go to London to complete the liquidation of Uncle Kilmer's estate. London was the original home of Kilmer's deceased wife, and his in-laws had put up barriers to all funds based in the city. Kilmer was twenty years his wife's senior, yet another scandal for the family years before, and his English Protestant in-laws would demand and keep much of the money left by Elizabeth, their deceased daughter. They were influential in London and did this out of spite for the man who stole her away.

Finn's absence in London left him unaware of his bride's long-standing plans for her marriage. He believed that they were still in the honeymoon phase, and he was not suspicious in any way, thinking that Carrie would feel just the same way he did. Were they not to live happily ever after? Wouldn't they grow old together?

After nine months, Carrie gave birth to a son, Ryms, and quickly placed him with a trusted nurse whom she hired for passage to America. The nurse was paid a salary befitting a princess and was sure to keep her lips sealed about any misgivings she might have over this arrangement.

Uncle Kilmer's first thought about Carrie proved true: she was out to find a husband, hoping to get away from her parents and to make a new life. Finn was her ticket out. He would pay a price for being enchanted by Carrie's beauty. Naiveté was his enemy. He saw only the good in people and never understood how anyone could be intentionally cruel to another, especially after professing love and making a lifetime commitment to that person. Carrie was a beauty on the outside and a beast on the inside.

Finn would find out the hard way that his bride was not who she appeared to be. She kept up a front to acquire money, then get as far away from Finn as she could. Carrie understood that money was the key, and she held all of the funds that came from Finn's beloved Uncle Kilmer.

With most of the funds from the inheritance in her hands, Carrie secured passage with immigrant smugglers to America. The boat waited for her and others off the coast of Castletownberre. Finn did not learn until too late of Carrie's conniving. She appeared sweet and in love with him, but in reality she was sly as a fox and out for herself.

Carrie also had Ryms, whose birth was known only to Carrie's inner circle by the day of her passage to America. Certainly, her husband was not part of that circle.

CHAPTER 6

Vanished: Double-Cross Carrie

CARRIE slipped off to America from the town of Finn's family, the family that he had fled several years before. Castletownberre folk had no clue as to Carrie's connection with the local-born Finn. She found passage to America with the funds she stole from him. The money would spare her a life in Ireland. It was the land of her birth, yes, but not where her heart was. Carrie's heart was not easily broken, and she saw

Carrie

no risk in hurting Finn. Her heart was not made of glass, as it seemed Finn's was. She would never regret doing what she did, and felt her actions justified as part of love and war. Finn came at the right time and the right place for her. She saw an opportunity and took it.

Returning to Dublin from London, Finn found that his wife had vanished along with his inheritance. He had no reason to remain in Dublin. He had no roots there, but he did not want to return to his sisters.

Finn was not yet nineteen. He had failed, having lost both his fortune and his love. Finn heard from the locals that Carrie had gone to Boston. She had been in correspondence for several years with a friend from Dublin who had moved there. Carrie would marry this Irish immigrant, but it was not a happy union. She entered this second union as a way to stay in America and didn't have love in mind. She was just as devious as she had been in her first marriage. Finn would eventually get word about his son, Ryms. This double loss and double cross brought him sorrow that he thought he would never overcome. Friends on his hurling team took to calling his runaway bride Double-Cross Carrie. Finn did not try to discourage them, though he was unable to voice his blessing for the epithet.

Finn took the small amount of money still in his possession and returned to London, breaking all ties with his native Ireland. He enlisted in the English navy and decided this would be his home for the rest of his life.

He wanted no part of any lass who would take his fortune, his heart, and his homeland. Finn felt that his only choice was to live life forever homeless, landless, and loveless aboard ships in the world's oceans. The sea would be his love, the stars would be his lights, and the ports of call would be the only places where he would plant his feet briefly on soil. He decided that this was a vow he would keep until his last breath.

Uncle Kilmer's elderly in-laws in London actually took a liking to the nineteen–year-old Finn after the courtesy and kindness he showed them. The couple wrote a letter of recommendation to secure a good posting for Finn in the English navy, and he enlisted for a career. This was a nice gesture by the couple, who had always seemed to have a distain for anything connected to Ireland. But the two loved Finn and saw him not as Irish but as a human being. Kilmer's in-laws would be Finn's new family, and they pledged that their home would be his whenever he was in England. They kept their vow until a house fire took them home to their daughter Elizabeth. Both were just shy of eighty. This was yet another loss for Finn.

Fate sent him to port after port across the globe. Finn was brokenhearted over Carrie's disappearance, distraught over his uncle's death, and homesick for

Sullivan Farm. The sun never set on the British Empire during Queen Victoria's reign, and he saw most of the world. But Finn's life felt empty. His love for Carrie would not fade. Finn felt as though he had an illness without a cure. Broken hearts do not always mend, and he thought his never would. On top of that, worrying about his son left him with a stomach ulcer that no medication could heal.

Finn traveled thousands of miles over the next few years. He was often at sea for weeks or months on end, gaining a wealth of skills, knowledge, and friends and recouping his funds. Finn captivated shipmates with his storytelling and became adept at cards. He also knew how to make wine and ale. Finn savored his mythical image. Shipmates knew a voyage without him would be like one without tea and biscuits. It just would not be the same.

Finn helped shipmates who partied a bit too much in port, navigating them back from the bars when they had forgotten who they were or where they were going. He had grown accustomed to life in the English navy, but he searched for an excuse to return home to Ireland. His heart still yearned for Carrie, but his love for his home-land was almost as strong. He figured he could satisfy that love without being hurt again.

The navy was in Finn's blood, as if seawater washed through his veins, instead of the red liquid. Word reached

Finn over the course of his port of calls, of deaths of kin. The deaths, he was told, were as if dominoes were falling in rapid succession among those whose blood did indeed flow through his veins.

The navy and the sea life that went with this were exchanged for land and the farm life.

Finn returned to Sullivan Farm when he got word during an Irish port call that several of his sisters had died over the past several years. He would stay forever after at the farm and never tell his surviving sisters of his marriage to Carrie, of his inheritance from Uncle Kilmer, of his misfortune in losing it, or of his son, Ryms. Finn simply told them that he had returned after learning that many of his siblings had passed away.

Finn pledged to his sisters that he was back for good and would follow orders, never again questioning their ways. They were thrilled at the return of their prodigal brother and giggled when he told them they were old cackling hens, but he wanted to come home to them anyway.

His sisters knew Finn as a brother long at sea who had returned with tales that might be a bit exaggerated but were entertaining as they sat around talking before bedtime. The sisters would hear differing versions of his sea tales but would always be spellbound and hang on every word he spoke. Finn never mentioned Carrie, Kilmer, or Ryms. That part of his time away from Sullivan Farm should be kept hidden, he decided. The local parish priest knew all of these secrets but would not tell a soul of Finn's other life. The two were buddies and often enjoyed a taste of Finn's brew or wine together. Finn let his heart speak only on these occasions, telling the priest of his lost Carrie and of the child he wished to see sometime before he met Saint Patrick in the afterlife.

Hanorah knew Uncle Finn as being full of stories but able to tend to the family farm better than any other villager might. Finn had saved some money from his navy years, and it would secure survival for him and his sisters as they aged. They were not wealthy, but they had the farm and what was upon it and would always prosper. They were blessed with food, with shelter, and with each other.

Hanorah understood that Finn had kept his past secret for his sisters' sake as well as his own. Reading his journal, she realized that it was wise never to judge anyone, since the person judged might someday be you.

Her two aunts would school Hanorah in the art of sewing clothes and blankets and cooking meals with the few ingredients available in Ireland during that era. They also encouraged her to read as much as possible. Deidre would often tell her that people could lose all of their possessions but could always keep their hearts and their minds. These two things would be lost only if a person chose to give them away.

Hanorah loved sewing, since she could make outfits for family members. She loved to cook, because she got to taste food unavailable at her own home, such as eggs. She also loved to read, and the hundreds of books at her uncle and aunts' house gave her the world outside of Castletownberre and Sullivan Farm in County Cork and Munster. Hanorah learned English and could speak it unself-consciously. Her uncle was more fluent in English than her two aunts and was a ready tutor for her.

Hanorah loved her times at Sullivan Farm. She fed the chickens, helped with the potato crop, tended to the vegetable gardens, and watched the livestock. The sheep and the goats became closer companions than her sister Katie.

Katie was more of an indoor person and did not like to get dirty. Hanorah loved the smell of the outdoors; the scent invigorated her and gave her inner strength. Katie did not share her nature. She preferred helping her aunts inside the house. Sewing and napping were her passions. She was not much for playing with critters like goats and sheep and chickens, for weeding the garden, or for working with vegetation of any type. Katie was especially relieved that there were no bugs in her uncle and aunts' home.

The insect-free environment was due to Aunt Keira's constant scrubbing and her debugging prowess. She was well known among villagers, who often tapped her knowledge. There were no fleas or bedbugs in her home. No one had to sleep on straw over dirt floors. There were beds. This home was a paradise, Hanorah thought. She was in heaven itself. The two aunts were peculiar in some ways, but fortunately one of their eccentricities was an obsessive cleanliness.

Hanorah befriended the goats and the sheep and made the animals her audience as she sang Irish tunes or read stories from the many books she consumed while at Sullivan Farm. She sometimes enlisted the goats and the sheep for the plays she would stage, the livestock substituting for human characters. A few other children spent time at the farm, and Hanorah made do with what she had and was always happy. Life is what you make of it, and you can make a good life with little if you try. You can do this if you are content at heart.

Hanorah loved Sullivan Farm, but she knew she had to return Sunday evenings to Castletownberre, to her *an chlann*, or family. She knew that her *ma'thair* and *athair*, her mother and father, needed her desperately. And she needed them.

Aunt Keira and Aunt Deidre prayed to Saint Bridget that their niece would one day become a schoolteacher. They knew that many young women relocated to America with the promise of employment as teachers. Women in

Munster left by the dozens in search of teaching jobs and also hoped to find marriage on the other side of the *aige'an*, or ocean. Teaching would be their ticket out of Ireland. Teaching would mean hope, and possibly a husband, for Hanorah.

Chapter 7

Holy Card, Shamrock, Letter

AUNT Keira and Aunt Deidre had themselves dreamed of America. Their kin, Barry, had made the trip when famine, *an gorta mor*, swept the land. He had only a holy card with Saint Patrick upon it, a shamrock, and a letter of invitation from an Irish immigrant family in Indianapolis that needed help.

Barry was kin to Aunt Keira and Aunt Deidre as cousins. Barry was a cousin by calling, one of the two aunts dozens of cousins in the extended family.

Barry received the letter through the intercession of a parish priest, Father Fergus, who had taken a liking to him early on. As a youngster, Barry shined above the other children. Father Fergus understood that the boy's energy and enthusiasm could only help him and that if the lad found a way out of poverty and out of Ireland he could be a catalyst for others to escape. His success could give hope to others. The priest knew that his congregation prayed to Saint Patrick for help and that more than a few wanted to leave Ireland for America. The shamrock was a symbol of hope that many a villager would carry across the Atlantic Ocean.

Barry was promised free room and board in exchange for corralling and managing the family's eight boys on Saturdays while the parents attended social gatherings. He was also promised an apprenticeship in the family's growing lumber company. The words *rowdy, unruly, ill-mannered*, and *cantankerous* were omitted from an account of these boys. Someone would later charitably describe them as "high-spirited."

Indianapolis was not Boston or New York City, but it was America, and Barry knew he must take advantage of the invitation. The eight boys would perhaps like the sport of hurling, he thought. He could coach them and burn off some of their energy, keeping them out of mischief.

Barry was not yet sixteen. He was suited for the trip to America, though he knew the voyage would be difficult aboard a ship carrying five times the number of passengers it was intended to hold.

People were crammed onto the deck and into lower rooms. The ship had little sanitation, and the odor made many passengers sick. Food was scarce, and the cramped conditions brought frequent illness. Barry was strong, healthy, youthful, and tough of spirit. He figured he was blessed to be aboard. Father Fergus had given Barry a holy card as he walked his young parishioner to the ship. On the back of the card, the priest had written in Gaelic, "Barry, Saint Patrick too was a stranger in a strange land. Be not afraid and your Irish blood will run strong in your veins and give you strength in America." The holy card did just what Father Fergus had envisioned: Barry would survive the passage to America in good health and in good spirits and with a strong soul.

Barry had made money for steerage to America by peddling food on the streets, but he often wasted the funds in evening contests with friends at the local tavern. The Irish American family would cover his passage in a promissory note. However, Barry wanted to earn money and be less in debt to his patrons. He regretted blowing his profits at the tavern.

Preparing for long days out at sea, the fishermen along Castletownberre's wharves bought potatoes, eggs, and bread each day at Barry's stand. He could have made a decent living and gained some security peddling food, but this would never have pleased him. He had dreams of wealth, and it would never come his way as a wharf peddler. He knew life in America offered a better opportunity.

Late one Sunday evening, Aunt Keira sat Hanorah and her sister down to talk. Aunt Deidre looked distressed. The girls were not normally at Sullivan Farm this late in the evening on most Sundays. Uncle Finn would already have brought the wagon around from the barn and had the sisters bid farewell to their aunts. A burlap bag filled with food would be in the wagon along with a small treat for brother Rian. The food would take the Martleys through the rest of the week back home in the village. The routine would end this Sunday.

Katie was unaware of the tone change, but Hanorah had felt concern over something in Aunt Deidre's voice that evening. When Aunt Keira walked into the room and sat down, Hanorah braced herself for life-changing news. She saw an expression in her aunt's face that she had never seen before.

"Hanorah, you and Katie will not return to Castetownberre for a while. You both must stay here in Sullivan Farm a wee bit longer before returning to your *an chlann*."

"Is there anything wrong with Rian?" Hanorah asked her aunt Deidre.

"Well, child, Rian is sickly, as you know well," Deidre said. "Uncle Finn is going to your parents' house now to find a doctor who can try to help Rian before it is too late. The doctors will only take money or food, so Uncle Finn is taking both into town to barter. He is good at telling stories, so he will most likely find a doctor who will visit your mommy and daddy's house to see about Rian. Uncle Finn will talk the doctor's ears off while he takes him to check your brother's medical condition. We can only pray to our Saint Patrick and Saint Bridget to protect Rian."

Hanorah normally did not shed tears, since her many encounters with hurt and suffering had strengthened her spirit. Katie, however, was soon in tears and went upstairs to the room that the sisters shared. She cried herself to sleep.

Hanorah's red hair was tied back in a bun, and she pulled it out of the bun, letting it fall to its full length at her waist. Katie's hair was blonde and shorter and always well groomed prior to leaving Sullivan Farm. The elderly aunts made sure their nieces' hair was washed and stylish before their return home. This too had always been a routine.

Neither girl had spent many nights away from home, and only here at the farm would they feel safe if not with their parents in the one-room cottage. Over the years, Katie and Hanorah now and then stayed for longer periods at Sullivan Farm, always due to an illness in Castletownberre. This time, the sisters felt, the illness must be more severe than ever before.

Uncle Finn was gone for several days in Castletownberre, and upon his return, he had unsettling news. He told Hanorah and Katie that they would be enrolled at the Catholic parish school for now and that they would stay at Sullivan Farm from this day forward. "You two girls will live with Aunt Deidre and Aunt Keira and myself for now," he told his nieces.

The girls briefly hoped that Uncle Finn was only telling one of his stories and that he would say everyone was still well back at home. But it was not to be.

"Monday I will take you to school in the wagon, and the days after that, the two of you girls will walk to and from school daily," he said. The school was three miles away, and the walk was over dirt roads and well-traveled trails. The girls knew the route well.

Uncle Finn did not want to go into details about what had happened in Castletownberre. He did not yet have the courage or the strength to report the tragic events to his nieces. Never at a loss for words, Finn could not find them now.

Hanorah's father, Brendan, could not keep a job for long after the death of his first child. He worked at the copper mines only when extra hands were needed. When his health had been good, he had a steady job and regular income at the mines.

Brendan would stand outside the mines in his meager clothing in all weather conditions, hoping for work, and eventually he could not fight off the illnesses that plagued him and his family. Hanorah's mother, Bridget, did what she could to earn money and help support the family, sewing clothes for neighbors. However, as she lost one child, then a second, and nursed Rian daily, her health declined. She could not shake off the melancholy that shadowed her.

Aunt Keira would send herbs and potions to Bridget each week. The potions had been handed down in the family for decades and in past years seemed to be cure-alls for any illnesses. However, Bridget and Rian could not shake off their ailments, and Brendan's health grew worse.

Bridget's spirits sank further as her health declined, and she prayed to God, Saint Patrick, and Saint Bridget that Katie and Hanorah would stay immune to illness. The two girls somehow became stronger, gaining weight and growing taller. Bridget and Brendan and Rian grew weaker, lost weight, and developed frightening coughs. They lost ground as each sun rose in the morning and as each moon appeared at night.

Chapter 8

Chance at Survival

BRIDGET day by day, night by night, was certain that she, Brendan, and Rian were suffering the same illness that had taken Fiona and Lorcan several years earlier. Bridget thought this fact over and over, as if it was a nightmare to occur.

The two aunts begged Brendan and Bridget to move to Sullivan Farm so they could help the family and give their relatives a better environment. Brendan and Bridget were proud and thought they would be a burden. The Martleys' only concession was to allow Hanorah and Katie a chance at survival. Hanorah was forever grateful to her mother for giving her this privilege. She was glad her mother's pride did not get in the way of this act of love. Sullivan Farm was safe.

Hanorah's constant reading, both in Gaelic and in English, gave her a window into the world outside of Ireland. Her exposure to these books brought her fluency in English, something that would work in her favor in the not-too-distant future. Hanorah became a gifted student at the Catholic school, and the nuns saw in her a spirit not found in many children under their care. She had an aura about her.

Hanorah was in the choir, and the nuns realized that she not only sang the hymns for Mass but also the songs she had written. They saw to it that she was given the time to write these songs down so others could hear them.

Uncle Finn would often say, *Eirinn go brach*, or "Ireland forever," but Hanorah could not get herself to repeat the words. After reading his journal, she understood how her uncle felt. He loved Ireland. She also loved her homeland, but she wanted to leave Ireland for a new world where there was plenty of food, plenty of shelter, sunny skies, and good health. Most of what Hanorah knew of the world came from books. Ireland was home to suffering, starvation, and deat h. There was good in Ireland, but there was also bad.

The area that Hanorah knew best, County Cork, was home, but not forever. Blarney Castle was her favorite landmark, but she dreamed of seeing the White House and the Capitol building in America. She lay awake some nights imagining how she would adapt to a new life there. Hanorah dreamed of riding on a train, attending an opera, and seeing a play. The books she read at Sullivan Farm showed that this was normal for many people in

America. Hanorah wanted this to become normal for her too. The phrase she used was "America forever."

The Atlantic Ocean was the only barrier, Hanorah thought, to a life in America. That and money to make the journey. The water barrier might as well be a million miles, and the funds needed might as well be a million dollars. She could surmount neither obstacle. That was the reality in the way of her dreams.

What Hanorah and Katie came to understand several weeks into their permanent stay at Sullivan Farm was that the rest of their family had perished.

Hanorah in youth

Uncle Finn had stayed with Rian, who died first, and then with Brendan and with Bridget. The three Martleys were buried in Castletownberre under Uncle Finn's sponsorship, and he returned to Sullivan Farm. He did not want the girls to suffer more heartache and could not bear to tell them of the family's fate. Each time the Martleys came up in conversation, Finn was quick to change the subject.

Finn and his sisters knew of Barry, now long established in America. Perhaps Barry could send the two girls

a letter of invitation to America. Finn would hate to lose these two darlings, but he knew their parents would want a better life for them. He wrote Barry a letter, asking him to sponsor the girls. Finn knew this would please them immensely.

Barry's reply would never arrive, but Sean's letter would. Sean was a onetime beau of Keira and had fled town while not yet out of his teens. He had heard from an Irish acquaintance of the letter sent to Barry. Sean invited Hanorah and Katie to come to New York City under his protection to become housekeepers and to as-

Katie in youth   sist at his restaurant. The sisters could earn their keep, pay off their passage to America, and then be freed to pursue their own lives.

Uncle Finn believed Sean to be sincere in his letter of invitation, and he wrote back accepting the promise of work for his nieces. The two were to be freed of all obligations when the elder sister, Katie, turned eighteen. That was the agreement.

Hanorah was now fourteen, and she thought she would work four years or so for Sean and then be on her own. The Martley girls set off from Castetownberre with new clothes sewn by their aunts, baskets full of food for the trip, thirty English pounds to serve them as a bankroll, and hope for a new life. The Ireland they loved was no longer to be their home. Hanorah also carried the sealed envelope from Uncle Finn's journal, the one marked "For America. To be opened by finder only."

Sean greeted the sisters upon arrival and at first treated them well. The girls were put to work in his Manhattan restaurant and labored twelve to twenty hours daily, seven days a week. Katie grew ill, and Hanorah wanted to set herself free from Sean's enslavement. This was not the America of her dreams. The sisters vowed that they would not be forced into a life of complete servitude.

After one year of this treatment, the Martley girls slipped out of Manhattan late one evening and set off for Indianapolis. There would be a friendly face from Castletownberre in Indianapolis, an old parish priest. Their aunts had mentioned him, and the sisters knew that this priest, now almost ninety, was wise and kind. He was known to help any of the Irish who visited his church, no questions asked. The priest was also privy to Finn's life story and knew the whereabouts of Ryms, who was unaware of the Martley girls or of any family connections from the past.

After listening to the girls detail their ordeal, the priest secured a place in a nearby convent where they could complete their schooling, perfect their reading and writing skills, and then hope for jobs through the nuns' intercessions. The convent gave the sisters a sense of permanence, a sense of pride, and a sense of security. The girls received a general education and lessons in religion, etiquette, and music from dawn to dark. However, the convent was not the life that either sister wished to pursue. Many girls living in the convent chose a religious vocation and offered their lives because they wanted to help others too. The Martley girls wanted marriage and hoped to be blessed with offspring.

On her arrival in Indianapolis, Hanorah had one possession from her childhood, something she had carried with her all the way from Castletownberre. It was a doll. Uncle Finn had pinned a note on it, telling her to read the message only in the event of an emergency.

Thinking an emergency had not yet occurred, Hanorah had left the note on the doll for more than a year. Finally she read the message, which said, "Please contact the Malones of des Moines, for they will help you." The note included an address, and this brought Hanorah and Katie new hope. The girls, who had not been exceptionally close, though they were always together, had only each other now and vowed to make sure that both would find good places to live. Hanorah felt that Saint Patrick and Saint Bridget were still standing by her side, guarding and guiding her. She had hope. And she still had her dreams. Katie also had dreams, though they were not the same as Hanorah's.

Hanorah gave the mother superior the note, and she made the contact. The Malones got Hanorah a job as a housekeeper outside of Des Moines and Katie a position tending to an elderly lady's seven orphaned grandkids in Indianapolis. A fellow named Ryms, a relative of the seven, lived in the home.

Hanorah had yet to open the envelope marked "For America. To be opened by finder only." This she would do only in the case of a final emergency, because this envelope might contain one last miracle for her in America.

CHAPTER 9

Find Her Dreams

THE two sisters' fates changed forever once they had left the convent.

Hanorah would find her dreams in a farm outside of Des Moines. Katie would find her dreams in Indianapolis. Their lives diverged once they had gone their separate ways. The sisters would have little contact from then on but were happy knowing that each would now have a prosperous life.

Katie would marry Shaun, an Irish lad, who had fortune and fame in his blood. Shaun put his considerable muscles and his brilliant mind to work. Both of these were his greatest assets and assured him with hard work he would succeed Katie and Shaun prospered and were wealthy from that time forward. Katie had been hired by Carrie, who never knew of their connection through Uncle Finn. Fate had dealt an artful hand. Katie would bear children and live a life rich in both love and money.

Carrie would only mend her ways after the loss of her son, Ryms. Ryms perished in a factory accident, just as many other Irish did so often. Carrie was said to never recover from this loss, and would die of a broken heart it was said.

Hanorah would meet Charles O'Donnell, an Irish lad with hair that looked like a carrot top when the sun shined upon it, sparkling eyes as green as shamrocks, and a personality that might have led some to suspect that Uncle Finn had produced an heir across the ocean. Hanorah worked for kin of Charles as a housekeeper on a neighboring farm. The hardworking farmer courted the twenty-year-old woman for about a year and won her heart. Charles was of 100 percent Irish stock. Hanorah thought she was blessed. How could she go wrong with an Irishman?

From her wedding day forward, Hanorah would be known simply as Nora. She prayed that her new life as a bride would be blessed and that she would produce healthy children. Nora sang Irish songs to her Charles, and with money received at her wedding, she bought pencil and paper to write down the lyrics to the songs she had composed over the years. The songs had been written only in her mind, and Nora wished the words to be kept for her legacy. The songs had seemed whimsical at the convent when the nuns heard her angelic voice and discovered her musical skills. Now they would be down on paper and could be enjoyed by others, including her children, Nora hoped.

Hanorah and Charles

Nora felt reborn, recharged, and ready to take on farm life and motherhood with Charles. He spent every hour possible laboring on the farm, and the hard work paid off with fruitful harvests. Nora was thankful to her uncle Finn and her aunts Deidre and Keira back home in Ireland. She wrote them monthly at first, but over the years the letters became too few as Nora grew busier and lost the art of writing in Gaelic. However, she never went one day without thinking of them. The three elderly relatives in Sullivan Farm felt blessed and proud that the Martley clan had gotten safely ashore and prospered in America.

Nora was blessed with children. They grew to hear her sing Irish tunes to them.

The farm provided a decent living for the family. The O'Donnells were not rich but were comfortable and were able to be respectable and self-sufficient.

The farm was what Nora had envisioned long ago in Ireland. She would hear her young children squabble and fight on occasion, just as any mother might. This was human nature; this was part of life. However, every evening as the sun began to set and candles were lit in the kitchen, the only room with nighttime light, Nora reminded her children that they should be forever thankful for the gifts they had in life. Nora would tell them, "Be thankful for the gift of life, the gift of health, the gift of love, the gift of food, the gift of shelter, the gift of clothes." Nora revealed very little about her childhood to her children, but they sensed that their mother must have been without many of the simple things that they took for granted.

Ada Jones, Billy Murray, and Edward Favor were Nora's favorite singers, the ones whose recordings she played on her Edison phonograph, although she longed for tunes from her homeland. Nora had plenty of food to eat and a farmhouse with wooden floors, and she knew her children would go on to live for decades. They were well fed, healthy, and full of the spirit exhibited by Aunt Keira, Aunt Deidre, and Uncle Finn. Irish blood was thick, and it flowed pure and unadulterated in their veins.

All of Nora's dreams seemed to have come true.

One evening in 1905, after the cry of a newborn baby was heard in the farmhouse, an Irish lullaby played softly on the Edison phonograph in Nora's room. She was thankful she had brought healthy children into the world, and she was thankful for the thirty years she had lived on earth. That was longer than either of her parents had lived, though only by a year or so.

The phonograph played the records that Nora had listened to over and over again. The music was medicine for the soul, she thought.

Nora was now once again Hanorah, and she was going home to Castletownberre to be reunited with Brendan and Bridget and Fiona and Lorcan and Rian. Hanorah knew the Martleys were waiting for her. Only Katie was not there, since she had many an Irish immigrant to help in Indianapolis before she would be called away. Hanorah would need to recall the tunes she sang to her parents as a girl young.

Rath de' ort.

Hanorah woke up with these words upon her lips each morning, just as she fell asleep whispering them. "The grace of God be with you."

Summoning every ounce of her fading strength, Hanorah asked Charles to retrieve the sealed envelope that she had discovered so long ago in Uncle Finn's journal. She mustered enough energy to open the envelope and found hundreds of English pounds. The funds would be a help to her family. Nora gasped for air and said her farewells to her husband and her children gathered around her bed.

Hanorah struggled for her last breaths. The young Irish girl was no longer starving, and there was plenty of every food available to fill her belly. This would be the normal circumstance each day from now on, and the girl and her family would get accustomed to living like this. They were now in the Castletownberre area of heaven. The little cottage was clean, and all of them were healthy. There were no more fleas on the floor or in the beds; there were no longer any bedbugs causing Hanorah to scratch throughout the night until she fell asleep bloody from itching; there were blankets for all family members now.

The Martleys were like many, many of their fellow townspeople and like many, many more of their country's citizens. Conditions had not been good, and many men had been out of work. Thus many families had lived each day with the threat of starvation and death.

They were now in heaven. Money was no longer a worry. Hanorah received a pencil from Saint Patrick and paper from Saint Bridget, and at last could finish writing down her Irish songs.

Hanorah drifted in and out of a dreamlike state of mind. She saw her mother and recalled how Bridget would often voice her hurt upon the deaths of friends and relatives, especially her children. She would only say that the deaths of her children were the hurts that would not go away. There was no antidote for this pain; no medicine, however strong, could extinguish it. Her losses left her with a melancholy that she could never shake. She would say that those who had entered heaven's gate at death were at peace and that those left on earth must endure the losses.

Hanorah thought lovingly of her mother, a person she never spoke of to her own children. She rarely shared the past with anyone, as if that phase of her life had somehow been erased.

Hanorah's daughter Anna brought the doll and placed it next to her mother. Daughter Mary asked her mother if she could see the doll. Daughters Teresa and Nora just looked at their mother lying there and told her she would feel better if she played with her doll. The doll. An Irish doll. A homemade gift from her grandmother long ago. One of Hanorah's few remaining links with Ireland, with childhood, only thirty years before but so long ago.

The doll had always held a place of honor in the kitchen cabinet and was off limits to any of Nora's children. Only now, as Hanorah lay dying, could the doll be brought out from the cabinet that had so long held it. The doll had a note pinned to it, and Hanorah had always been told that the note would one day be her personal guardian angel. Anna unpinned the note and read it out loud to her mother as Ada Jones played on the phonograph. On one side was the Malones' address, and on the other the phrase *Rath de' ort*. Hanorah would soon fall asleep peacefully forever.

Hanorah's four eldest children gathered around their mother and sang the Irish lullaby that she had often used to sing them to sleep. They sang in Gaelic.

Nora tried to whisper words to her children as she continued to fade. These were the instructions she had so often given them: You will sometimes fight among yourselves as any siblings will. However, every day in the evening, as the sun sets and the candles are lit, remember to be thankful for the breath of life. Thank God for the gift of life, the gift of love, the gift of food, the gift of shelter, and the gift of clothes.

The lullaby ended. She was now fast asleep. Her children knew that their mother would awaken to shamrocks, Saint Patrick, and the Ireland of her dreams. *Rath de' ort.*

Hanorah was an orphan no more, for she now saw her parents walking towards her as the music in the room gave way to the sounds of Irish lullabies at heaven's gates. Hanorah was now just as if she was that young girl in Ireland a lifetime earlier.

Rath de' ort.

Chapter 10

Life and Death and Heaven Too

As Hanorah gasped for one last breath and a final glimpse of her six children, someone took the statues of Saint Patrick and Saint Bridget from their honored kitchen perch and gingerly carried them into the bedroom.

These two statues were the same two saints that held that held that honored position in the Ireland of Hanorah's youth.

Mary, the eldest, went outside to the garden, lovingly tended to by their mother, and brought in several roses. The roses were yellow, white, red, and purple, and had green leaves, which Nora said reminded her of Ireland.

Anna reached into the kitchen cupboard for her mother's favorite vase, brought out only on the feast days of her honored saints, and filled it with water from the kitchen well. Teresa carefully took the chapel veil and rosary beads held in her mother's top dresser drawer and gave them to her dad. Charles stood alongside his bride of many years, silent except in the heart. He was not one to express emotion, especially before his young children, and mourned from within.

Nora, the youngest daughter, drifted around the room, playing with her doll, and trying to keep her two little brothers giggly with her silly and playful antics. The two brothers were Earl and Bud.

This was Hanorah's legacy: six young children left to forge for themselves in life. Mary, Anna, Teresa, Nora, Earl and Bud.

The local parish priest, Irish of course, made it out to the farmhouse by horseback, Bible in hand. Father entered the farmhouse, and went directly to the bedside of his long time parish member. Father understood from the scent of the angels that filled the room, Hanorah was at heaven's gate.

The Bible was opened, and the words from chapter thirty-five Sirach left Father's lips.

'He shows no partiality to the weak, but hears the grievance of the oppressed. He does not forsake the cry of the orphan, nor the widow when she pours out her complaint.'

As the breaths that Hanorah gasped grew weaker, Anna recalled that her mother treasured reading that biblical passage, as it soothed her heart.

The light that filled the Iowa farmhouse at Hanorah's last breath was not the glow of sunlight, the glow of candles, or even the glow from Edison's lightbulbs. Saint Patrick had flipped on the lights to the Ireland of Hanorah's dreams, with a shamrock in one hand and a potato in the other. Both were important. Both were symbols of her Ireland.

These were for Hanorah.

Hanorah, home at last.

Author's Note

My account of Hanorah's life is fact and fiction, inspired by family folklore and legend. Teresa O'Donnell Hill, Hanorah's third child, my grandmother, would talk of her mother as if she were still physically present. This was because her mother had been taken from her when she was only a child.

Hanorah was still with Teresa in her heart and in flesh and blood. Hanorah's life was what it had been to Teresa as a child, the facts embellished with the passing of her almost ninety-four years.

Hanorah lives on with this book and with the readers who learn of her life and times and of those she touched so long ago.

Praise God for Ireland and for those Ireland sent forth to America's shores.

I hope you enjoyed the story of my Irish great-grandmother. This story is a tribute to her and to the hundreds of thousands of Irish immigrants who crossed the

Atlantic Ocean in pursuit of a better life in the greatest nation on earth, the United States of America.

Rath de' ort.

This book was first published in softback version in 2012. I hope that readers will find the hard bound version a book to be cherished and that they also will remember their roots—where their people came from, where they have gone, and where they belong, no matter what their country of origin.

About the Author

Paul Brown is a fifth generation Houstonian, who worked for Fluor Corporation for twenty-five years and now works for a drilling company based in Houston, Texas. Paul graduated from the University of Houston, where he was a reporter for the 'Daily Cougar', worked for the Houston Post newspaper and was a legislative aide for the Texas House of Representatives. Paul has resided in Dhahran, Saudi Arabia; Ft. McMurray, Alberta, Canada; Rochester, New York; Mt. Clemons, Michigan; Wichita Falls, Texas; Irving, Texas and Ulsan, South Korea, and has worked in the United Arab Emirates.

Books by the author, Paul Brown

Orphan among the Irish: Hanorah's Story

Birdy the Backyard Blue Jay

Passing the Time

More Time to Pass

Still Another Time, Times Remembered

Best of Times

Times Now and Then, Then and Now

Thy Kingdom Come: Life of an Expatriate in Saudi Arabia

Birdy
the Backyard
Blue Jay
Wing Adventure

PAUL
BROWN

Passing The Time

Paul Brown

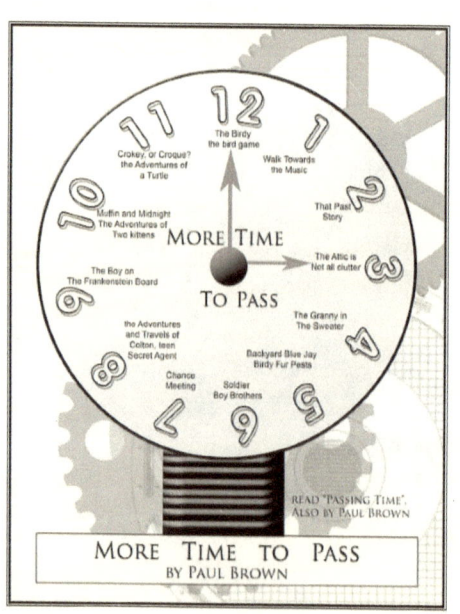

READ "PASSING TIME",
ALSO BY PAUL BROWN

MORE TIME TO PASS
BY PAUL BROWN

Still Another Time,
Times Remembered

Paul Brown

The Best of Times

Paul Brown

Photos and sketches are the property of the author.

www.ingramcontent.com/pod-product-compliance
Lightning Source LLC
Chambersburg PA
CBHW030357290526
45785CB00004B/1791

जैकम के पठ्यक्रम के दौरान, एक व्यक्ति के जैकम में वे क्रिसिस के चरणें के दौरान का अनुभव है कि संघर्ष के परिणाम के रूप में विभिन्न क्रिविसें क्रिसिस करत है. एक व्यक्ति के क्रिसिस के इन चरणें के दौरान घटित घटनओं है कि के अनुसर क्रिसिस करत है. एक स्वस्थ स्थिति में व्यक्तिगत संतुलन और क्रिसिस के महत्वपूर्ण चरणें के दौरान होत है कि संघर्ष के स्वस्थ समझ के स्तर को प्राप्त होग. एक अस्वस्थयकर स्थिति में व्यक्ति अक्सर व्यक्ति के लिए एक अनुरूही स्थिति य maladaptive संकल्प के लिए प्रदान करेग कि संघर्ष के चरम प्रस्तवें पर ध्यान दिय जएग.

इन प्रस्तवें से व्यक्ति के अन्ने जैकम और क्ह समज के संदर्भ में खद कैसे के एक दृश्य और उसके वतरण में महत्वपूर्ण है के रूप में क्य क्रिविसें क्रिसिस करत है. इन मन्यतओं व्यक्ति नय अनुभव और जैकम में

घटनओं के लिए उद्देश्य और अर्थ समझत है जिस तरह से प्रभावित करते हैं. व्यक्ति क्य है य क्य जैकन के किमास के चरणें में संकट संभल जिस तरीके पर आधारित बेमार किवसें का किमास हो सक्त है. इसके अलव, जैकन के एक वर्तमन य पिछले चरण व्यक्ति क्य य क्य वर्तमन जैकन में सम्मन कर रहत है क्य के लिए अर्थ य उद्देश्य के बरे में तर्कहीन विचारें को किमसित करने के लिए प्रेरित कर सक्त है.

बेमार सेच प्रक्रियओं को किमसित करने और एक व्यक्ति द्वारा बनए रख है कि कैसे की प्रक्रिय को समझने में उपचर रोग की न्हीं एक क्षेत्र को संबोधित लेकिन प्रक्रिय के सभी तीन पहलुओं को संबोधित पर ध्यन केंद्रित करन चहिए. यह संकेत किमास के विषय में उभर उठने की

-2-